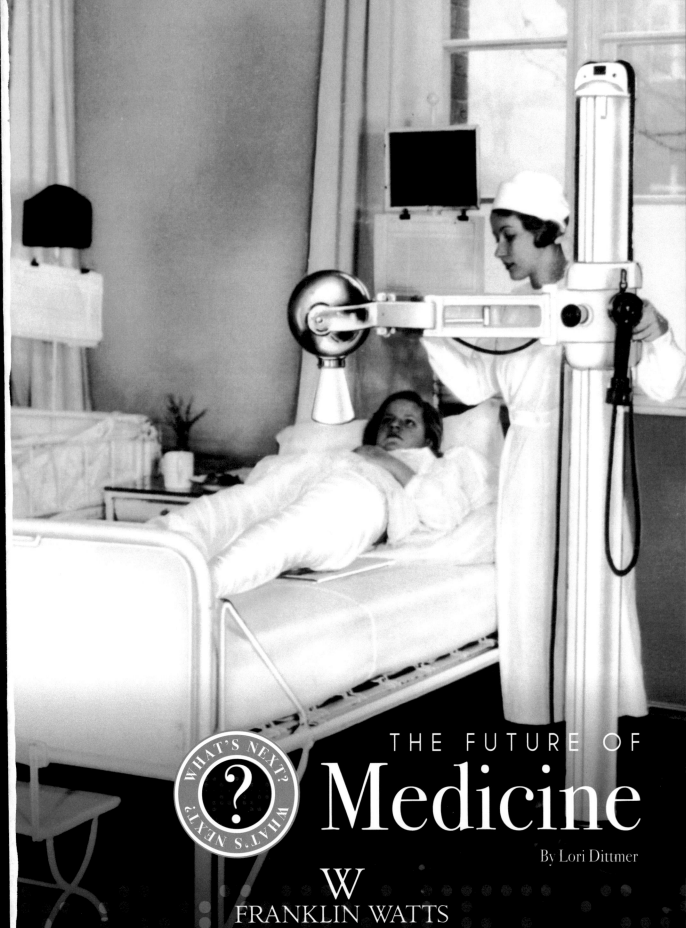

THE FUTURE OF
Medicine

By Lori Dittmer

W
FRANKLIN WATTS
LONDON•SYDNEY

WHAT'S NEXT? WHAT'S NEXT?
?

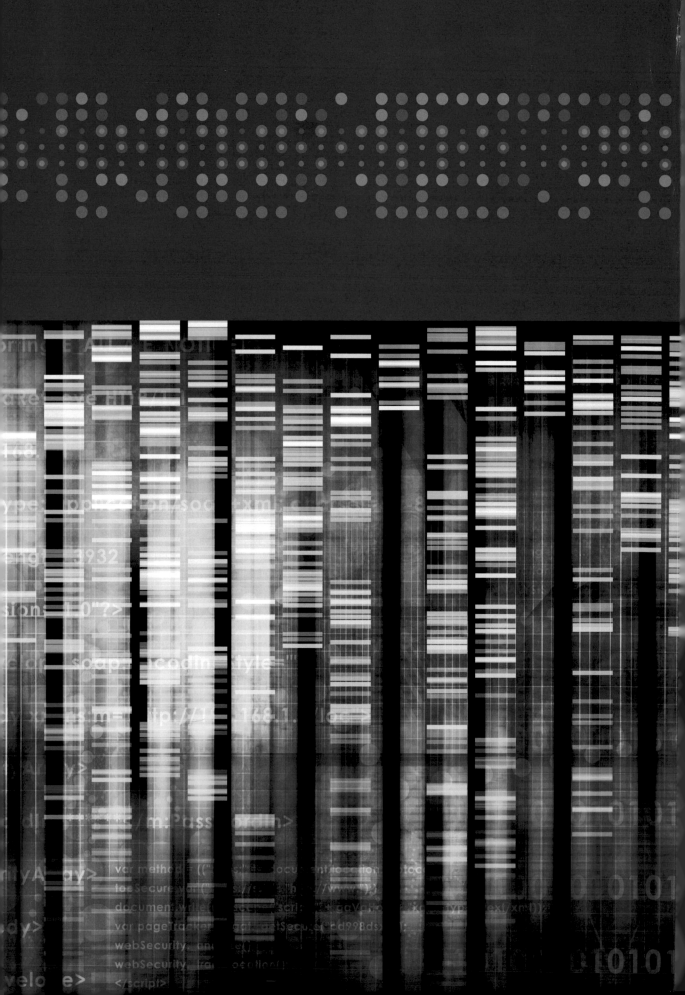

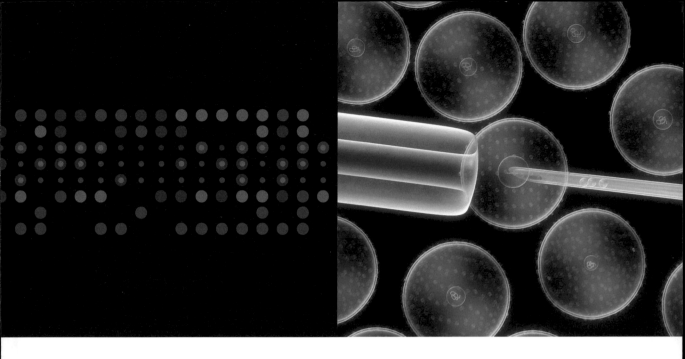

Contents

INTRODUCTION

What if you could have a medical check-up without visiting a doctor? Imagine simply touching your finger to a small device that draws a tiny amount of blood and promptly runs 2,000 different tests. The device sends the results to a computer, which sorts through a vast amount of information about your blood, organs, genes and the way in which the environment is affecting your body. The results are emailed to you and your doctor. Check-up complete. Next, the doctor looks at the data from your blood to see whether you are at risk of developing certain health problems. Then, he or she might prescribe medicine to help prevent these conditions from developing.

Such a medical check-up seems far-fetched today, but as technology improves, we might indeed be able to undergo medicals that are that quick and thorough. Throughout history, doctors and scientists have steadily improved medical treatments, from killing germs and developing disease-fighting drugs to performing life-saving surgery. A century ago, most people probably would not have believed that doctors would ever be able to transplant organs such as kidneys, hearts and livers from one person to another. But the knowledge necessary for these operations accumulated quickly during the 20th century, suggesting the likelihood of more great leaps in the next century. Although we'll have to settle for visits to the GP surgery for a while, a future of personalised medicine – in which a patient receives treatment according to the data provided by his or her own blood – awaits.

Medical experts predict a future in which doctors will be able to 'read' a person's cells (illustrated, above) and DNA (illustrated, right) to better anticipate health problems.

DISCOVERING GERMS, DEVELOPING DRUGS

Medical treatment among the earliest civilisations often involved sorcery and the supernatural. People blamed evil spirits for causing ill-health. Archaeologists have found ancient skulls showing evidence of trepanation, a procedure in which holes are drilled into a living person's skull. Although this surgery has been used in more modern times to relieve pressure from internal bleeding inside the skull, researchers believe that early doctors performed trepanation to release evil spirits from patients suffering from headaches, fits or mental illness. In India, surgeons sometimes concluded operations with the help of large Bengali ants. After surgery, the doctor would place the ants next to each other at the site of an incision. After the insects had clamped their powerful jaws down on the patient's skin, the doctor cut away the ant bodies, leaving the heads as stitches that eventually dissolved.

Ancient societies also used plants to treat illnesses. Medicine men who used these plants probably didn't know why certain plants helped specific ailments but could observe how people felt after eating the plants. Opium and black cohosh were found to ease pain, while figs were effective laxatives. Aloe vera helped to soothe skin conditions and pomegranate killed parasitic worms in the intestines. These plants contain powerful healing substances, and many of today's drugs still include their ingredients. Ancient Egyptians were particularly skilled at using plants for healing people. In fact, the word

The natural world continues to be a source of plant medicines – including pomegranate (left) and aloe vera (below).

Anton van Leeuwenhoek has been called the 'Father of Microbiology', as his observations of bacteria, tiny blood vessels and more opened new doors in medicine.

'chemistry' comes from an old Greek name for Egypt, *Khemia*, or 'land of black earth', so-called because of the fertile, crop-growing region found along the River Nile in Egypt.

For thousands of years, people remained unaware that living in dirty, crowded conditions directly contributed to health problems, and diseases such as leprosy, smallpox and dysentery – an illness that causes severe diarrhoea – were rampant. In the 1300s, a deadly disease called bubonic plague swept through Europe out of central Asia. The plague, which causes severely swollen lymph nodes, also known as buboes, stems from bacteria that live in the stomachs of fleas that feed on the blood of rats or other rodents. People develop the disease after being bitten by infected fleas, by handling animals with the disease, or by coming into contact with a person carrying it. The insanitary living conditions in cities throughout much of Europe brought many people into close proximity with fleas and rats, and the plague became an epidemic. From 1347 to 1351, the plague, also called the Black Death, killed 25 million people, or about one in every four people in the world. Doctors believed the best treatment for the plague was bloodletting, using leeches to drain blood from ill patients.

By the 1500s, scientists began to speculate that diseases were caused by tiny living creatures too small to see. An Italian doctor named Girolamo Fracastoro studied various diseases, including

THE MICROSCOPE SHEDS NEW LIGHT

Historians often credit Hans and Zacharias Janssen, father and son spectacle makers from the Netherlands, with the invention of the microscope. In the 1590s, they noticed that objects appeared much closer when a person looked through two carefully shaped lenses in a straight line. This tool magnified objects 3 to 10 times, allowing researchers to view human tissue, cells and the germs they had speculated about but could not previously see. Today, light microscopes, which use light to assist in the magnification, can enlarge views of tissue and blood samples up to 2,000 times. The most powerful of all are electron microscopes, which use beams of electrons – the negatively charged particles in atoms – instead of light to produce magnifications of a million times or more.

smallpox, cholera and the plague. In 1546, he suggested that tiny organisms, which he called 'disease seeds', were responsible for illness. Fracastoro believed they could spread sickness through direct contact, through contaminated food or clothing, or through the air. Although his ideas were widely praised by scientists for a short time, his disease seeds were then largely forgotten.

More than 100 years later, Dutch naturalist Anton van Leeuwenhoek made an important discovery. He was not a doctor or a trained scientist, but he enjoyed grinding glass lenses, making microscopes and using them to look at small objects such as strands of hair and insect wings. Van Leeuwenhoek noticed tiny animals swimming in a single drop of water and he called the creatures 'animalcules'. He began to write letters about his findings to the Royal Society of London, a prominent group of scholars who discussed scientific matters. In one 1683 letter, van Leeuwenhoek detailed an experiment in which he took some plaque from his teeth and from four other people and compared the samples. "I then most always saw, with great wonder, that in the said matter there were many very little living animalcules, very prettily a-moving," he wrote in what was likely the first description of bacteria. Despite this huge medical discovery, scientists did not realise that animalcules had any connection to disease.

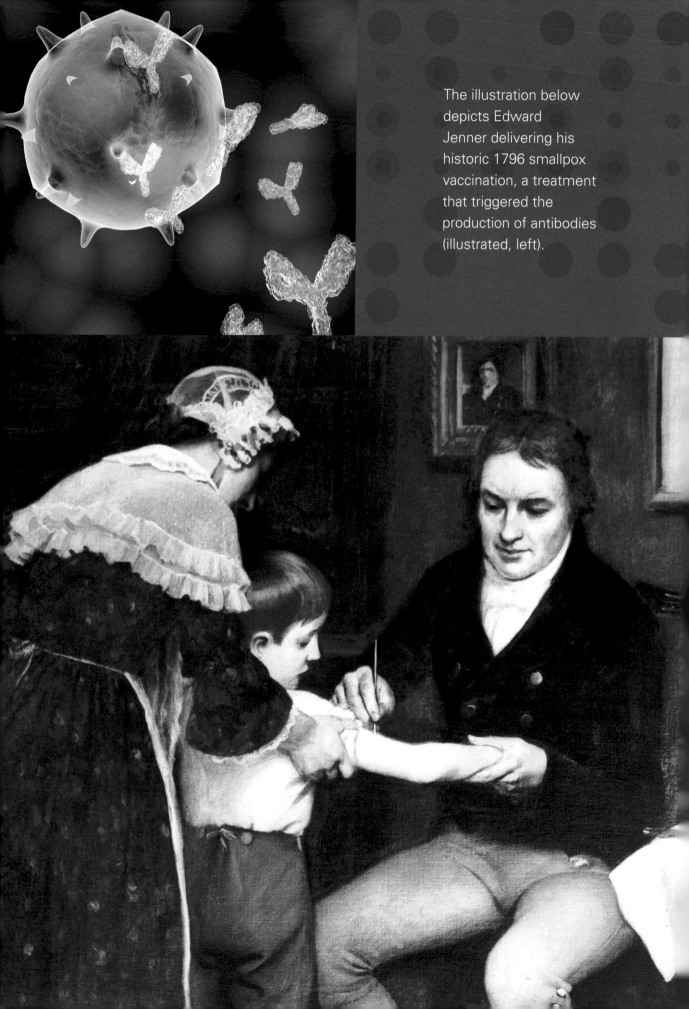

The illustration below depicts Edward Jenner delivering his historic 1796 smallpox vaccination, a treatment that triggered the production of antibodies (illustrated, left).

In 1796, an English doctor named Edward Jenner administered the first recorded vaccination to prevent a disease. Smallpox was a highly contagious and often lethal disease marked by chills, fever, hallucinations and pus-filled sores. As a country doctor, Jenner had treated milkmaids for cowpox, a milder form of smallpox that was common in cows. The milkmaids contracted the disease from milking infected cows, but Jenner noticed that once they had recovered from cowpox, the women did not develop smallpox. Jenner drew pus from the sore of a patient with cowpox and injected it into the son of a local farmer. The boy developed cowpox and, after he recovered from the disease, Jenner intentionally infected the boy with smallpox. The boy did not develop smallpox. Although Jenner could not explain why his experiment worked, we now know that immunisations, which contain a dead or weakened form of a disease, cause a person's body to produce antibodies. These antibodies fight off the invading germs, and if the germs return, the antibodies recognise them and fight them again.

Finally, in the 1800s, several researchers began drawing connections between van Leeuwenhoek's animalcules and disease. Both French scientist Louis Pasteur and German doctor Robert Koch studied germs of various diseases, including anthrax, and worked to develop vaccines. A Hungarian doctor named Ignaz Semmelweis worked at a teaching hospital, where students would study corpses – getting blood on their hands and coats – and then go

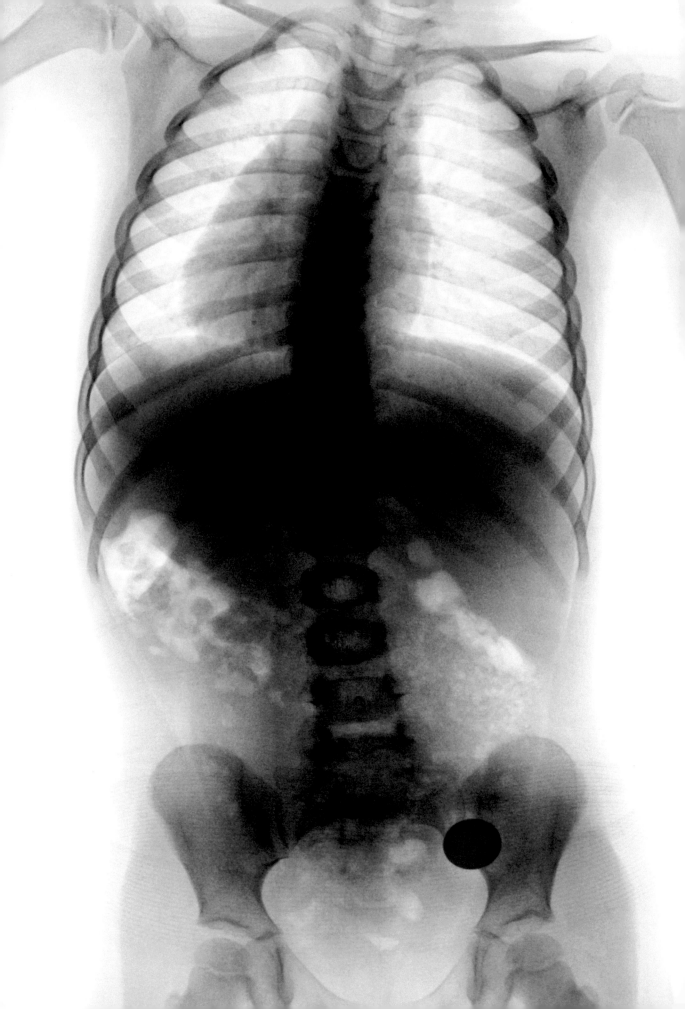

With X-rays, skeletal problems and foreign objects are shown clearly, as the images reveal the extent of bone breaks (right) or the location of a swallowed coin (opposite).

directly to the maternity ward to deliver babies. In 1847, nearly one third of the women who gave birth in hospital developed an infection called childbed fever and died within a few days. Semmelweis came to believe childbed fever could be prevented if the doctors thoroughly washed their hands before visiting each patient. Indeed, once the routine was implemented, the rate of infection dropped dramatically.

As more germs, viruses and bacteria were identified, researchers were able to develop medicines to fight them. Vaccinations helped prevent diseases, and antiseptics killed germs on doctors' hands and on medical instruments. Other drugs, such as penicillin, helped people recover from infections. Improved methods of preventing infection allowed doctors to perform operations more safely, with less risk of spreading germs to the patient's wound or internal organs. In 1895, German physicist Wilhelm Roentgen discovered a kind of electromagnetic radiation that he called X-rays. He found that these currents passed through soft tissues in the body but were blocked by bones and other hard surfaces. This discovery gave doctors a way

CENTURIES OF SYRINGES

Syringes – devices consisting of a piston inside a hollow cylinder – have been used in medicine for centuries. A book written by Greek inventor and mathematician Hero of Alexandria in the first century CE describes the use of syringes that can push out air or liquid. In ancient Greece, doctors used syringes mainly for drawing pus from boils and infected wounds; in fact, the Greek name for the syringe, pyulkos, means 'pus puller'. In the 1800s doctors began to use syringes to inject medicinal drugs into a patient's tissues or muscle. Today, doctors and nurses use syringes every day to draw blood, give immunisations or inject other medicinal drugs.

to see inside a patient's body to detect broken bones or any foreign objects, such as swallowed coins.

By the early 1950s, surgeons had operated on hearts, brains and other major organs. The next advancement was organ transplantation – taking a healthy organ from one person and putting it inside a patient with a damaged or diseased organ. The first major organ transplants were done with kidneys, because although humans have two, they can live with just one functioning kidney. In the earliest cases, the kidney recipient began recovering after surgery, only to get ill again. British researcher Peter Medawar discovered that the problem was a physical reaction of the body called rejection. Patients receiving tissues from another person formed antibodies to fight off the new tissue, and the transplants failed. Joseph Murray, an American surgeon, confirmed this idea in 1954 when he performed a kidney transplant involving identical twin brothers. Because of their shared DNA, the twin's immune system did not see the donor organ as foreign, and the transplant was a success.

Researchers then sought ways to help a patient's body accept foreign tissues. The drug cyclosporine was introduced in the 1970s as an effective immunosuppressant, a drug that prevents a patient's body from rejecting foreign tissue. Since then, kidney transplants have become safe and common procedures, paving the way for other organ transplant surgery.

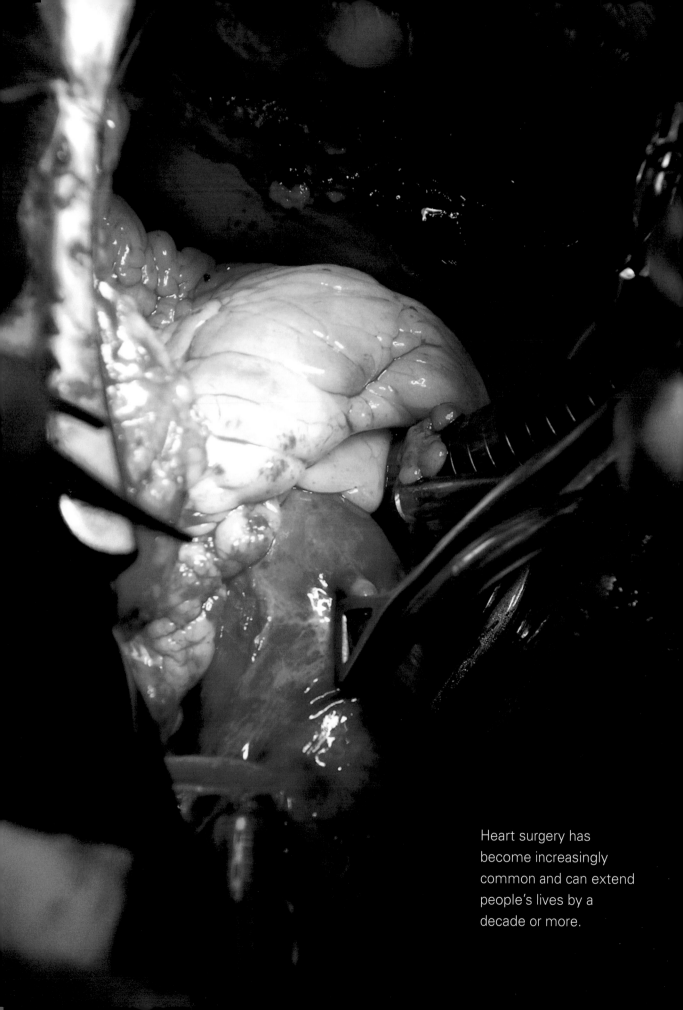

Heart surgery has become increasingly common and can extend people's lives by a decade or more.

TAKING THE FIGHT INSIDE

In recent years, scientists have been studying cells and genes, the building blocks of our bodies, to find ways to cure diseases and extend lives. Researchers are also making progress in using robots to perform surgery and in using computers to help restore such functions as vision and physical movement in patients.

Researchers are particularly interested in stem cells. The human body is made up of billions of microscopic cells. We have blood cells, brain cells and muscle cells, with each type performing a different job. If these cells die, they might not be replaced, and if too many cells die, that part of the body will be damaged. Stem cells are cells that can repair damage within our bodies by assuming the role of any kind of cell. For example, the stem cells in our skin replace skin cells damaged by a cut or sunburn. We can donate blood because the stem cells in our bone marrow will replace the lost blood cells. Researchers are trying to work out how to take these stem cells and put them in another person's body as a means of cell replacement. For years, doctors have performed bone marrow transplants, taking marrow cells from a healthy donor and putting them into a patient whose marrow is not working properly or has been damaged by invasive treatments such as chemotherapy. Scientists believe stem cells can help the body repair itself, enough to recover from a variety of diseases. However, stem cells taken from adults are generally only able to repair the

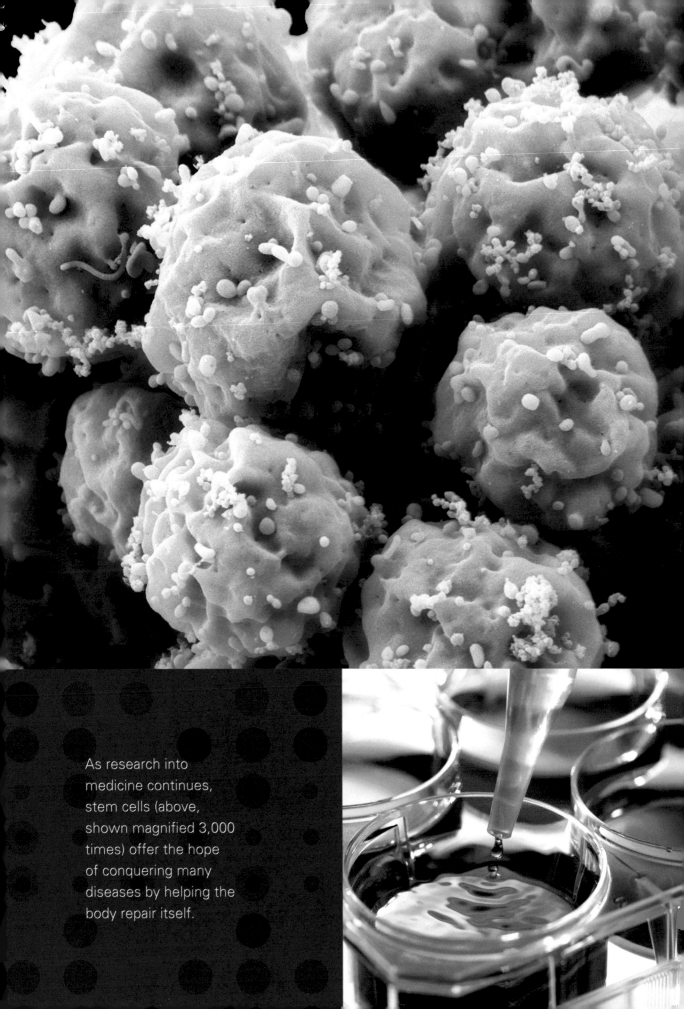

As research into medicine continues, stem cells (above, shown magnified 3,000 times) offer the hope of conquering many diseases by helping the body repair itself.

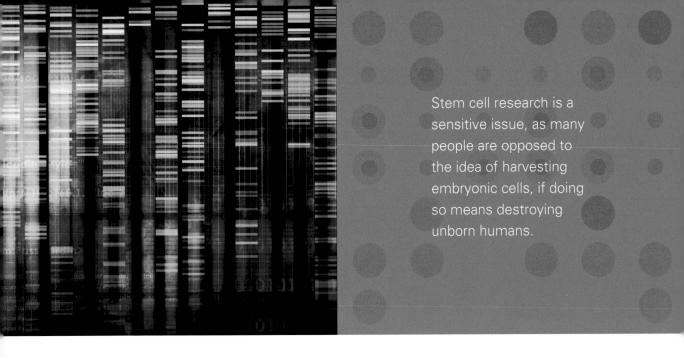

Stem cell research is a sensitive issue, as many people are opposed to the idea of harvesting embryonic cells, if doing so means destroying unborn humans.

same part of the body that they were taken from.

Researchers have found a more adaptable stem cell in embryos, which are unborn humans in the very earliest stages of life. These embryonic stem cells have the potential to become any kind of cell, which has opened up possibilities for treating many diseases, including Alzheimer's disease, Parkinson's disease and multiple sclerosis, which currently have no cure. Doing research with embryonic stem cells is highly controversial. Scientists obtain embryos from fertility clinics that would otherwise discard them because they no longer need them, and the harvesting of stem cells destroys the embryo. Many people oppose such stem cell research, believing it is morally wrong to deliberately destroy living embryos. Others fear that, in the future, the use of embryonic stem cells might lead to people buying and selling embryos as 'repair kits'. Those in favour of the research point to the possible benefits – conquering diseases and prolonging healthy lives.

Scientists are not only looking at transplanted cells as a means of fighting disease; they are also studying the 'instructions' within cells. These instructions, called genes, form long strands of deoxyribonucleic acid, better known as DNA. Genes are hereditary and determine many aspects of our bodies, including eye colour, hair colour, height and whether we are likely to develop certain diseases. In 2003, researchers for the Human Genome Project announced that they had fully mapped out the human genome – the roughly 20,500 genes in the human body. During the first decade of the 21st century, technology for genetic analysis improved, making the mapping process faster and cheaper.

Because of these advances, private companies can offer customers an analysis of their genetic map. At the moment, this testing can reveal whether patients have an increased risk of developing diseases – for example, a specific type of cancer – that run in families. Genetic testing can indicate if chemotherapy is likely to help certain cancer patients. The test can even show whether a patient's cancer is likely to come back, or whether he or she has the gene for rare hereditary diseases. However, scientists say that, at present, the benefits of genetic mapping – which can be costly – are limited and won't lead to improved treatment for the average person. "Admittedly, right now your family history may be your best bet, and it doesn't cost anything," said Francis Collins, former director of the US National Human Genome Research Institute.

Recent breakthroughs in medicine have also included ways to merge humans with machines to save and improve lives. In 2010, a

DYS DYS DYS DYS DYS DYS DYS DYS DYS D
5a 385b 388 389I 389II 390 391 392 393 426 438 43
13 13 13 30 24 11 13 13 12 12 1

DNA research sheds light on the ways in which traits – and potentially diseases – are shared within families (pictured, a woman [far left], her mother and her son).

Medical advancements have been saving and improving lives for centuries, and people who become doctors aim to help individual patients and society as a whole. From advocating the use of clean water to developing immunisations and life-saving operations, researchers have helped people to live longer. Around 400 CE, when the Roman Empire was ending, the average life expectancy was roughly 30 years. Although some people lived long lives, many died during infancy or childhood. In some developed countries, life expectancy has risen from 57 years in the early 1900s to more than 80 years today.

43-year-old American named Charles Okeke received the first portable artificial heart machine, which runs on batteries and weighs about 5.9 kilogrammes. Before the operation, Okeke was connected to a 181-kilogramme machine that kept his heart pumping, but improvements in technology allowed researchers to make a small device with enough power to support the heart. Okeke's ventricles – the two main chambers of the heart responsible for pumping blood to the entire body – and four of his heart valves were removed, and tubes connected the artificial heart in his chest to a power pack that he carried on his back.

A growing trend in modern surgery is to use robotics to assist the surgeons. In the early 2000s, doctors began using robotic surgical systems to perform operations on the heart, brain, prostate and other body parts. In robotic surgery, several robotic arms, with operating instruments attached, are in the operating room with the patient. A human surgeon sits in a different room, controlling the arms and instruments via remote controls while watching the procedure on a monitor. Canada's McGill University Health Centre took robotic surgery even further in October 2010 when robotic arms, controlled by doctors, both administered the anaesthetic and performed an operation in which a patient's prostate was removed. Experts say that robotic surgery offers many benefits over operations performed purely by human hands.

This photo shows a close-up look at the 'hands' of the *da Vinci* Surgical System – a robotic machine that gives surgeons precise control and involves minimal cutting in patients.

In 2006, American Claudia Mitchell – who lost her left arm in a motorcycle accident – received the first complex bionic arm, which was 'wired' into her nerves.

They are programmed to make specific cuts, and their 'hands' will never shake or cut too deep. Surgical robots can also operate through smaller incisions, which improves patient safety and allows for faster recovery after the procedure.

The portable heart and the robotic surgeon are two ways in which machines have improved medicine. Another way is through bionics, or the use of mechanical and computerised systems to help patients regain lost movement, vision and hearing. In the past, people who lost an arm or leg might be given a wooden, metal or plastic prosthesis to take the place of the missing limb. But now, scientists are developing neural prostheses, which respond to commands from the patient's brain.

When people have a limb amputated, or removed, they may feel as if the arm or leg is still there. This feeling is called a phantom limb. In fact, the nerves leading to the lost limb are still alive but disconnected. Todd Kuiken, a doctor and biomedical engineer at the Rehabilitation Institute of Chicago, USA, found a way to reroute these signals to different groups of muscles. Sensors in a neural prosthesis are positioned over these muscles and are programmed to recognise the signals for particular movements. Then, the artificial arm sends the signals to a motor that drives mechanised parts to move the fingers, bend the elbow or turn the wrist.

A MEDICAL MISTAKE

Improved medical treatment prevents people from getting ill and reduces the number of deaths from illnesses and injuries. But sometimes, new treatments can harm as well as help. In the 1950s, American scientist Jonas Salk developed a vaccine to protect people against polio, a disease that can cause paralysis and death. The vaccine was a success and was mass-produced to inoculate schoolchildren. After the vaccination programme began, some of the children fell ill. Researchers discovered that a laboratory in the state of California had not prepared the vaccine correctly. Although the vaccine protected thousands of children from polio, 200 developed the disease and 11 died.

Kuiken performed the procedure on Amanda Kitts, a woman who had lost the lower part of her left arm in a car accident, in 2006. "It was wonderful," Kitts said. "It made me feel more human because I could work it almost like a regular arm. I just had to think and it responded. My new arm made me feel like I could do anything again." While the human arm has more than 22 points of movement, a modern neural prosthesis can make only seven movements. But in the next phase of development, researchers are hoping to create an arm capable of all 22 natural movements.

Researchers are also looking at computerised methods of restoring vision in people with degenerative eye diseases. After more than a decade of study and testing, scientists have come up with a way to use a tiny video camera and a computer to transmit video signals to 60 electrodes attached to the surface of the patient's retina, or the nerve layer that senses light at the back of the eye. This technology has not yet restored perfect vision, but it has allowed patients to see the outlines of objects again.

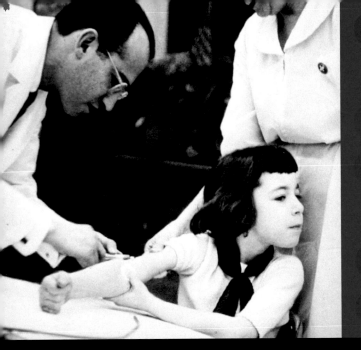

The polio vaccinations delivered by Jonas Salk (left) were a form of preventive medicine, while eye operations (below) represent corrective medicine.

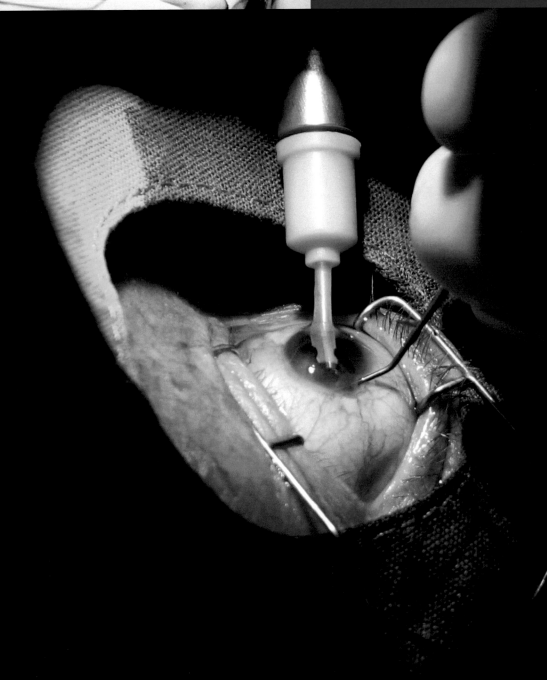

CELLS AND SMALL SURGEONS

When you imagine how medical procedures and treatments of the future may look, think small. By the middle of the 21st century, many treatments might work from the inside of the body in the form of new drugs and tiny robots that perform internal surgery. Such developments may make operations that require doctors to cut open the patient obsolete. For the most part, future medical advances will be aimed at keeping patients well rather than seeking out and reacting to diseases and disorders – prevention rather than cure.

Genetic testing will become more common as the price drops. Eventually, researchers predict, it will cost less than a hundred pounds to map a person's genome in hours or minutes, compared with the £1.9 billion ($3 billion) it cost for the first one to be completed from 1990 to 2003. It is quite possible that acquiring a complete genome sequence for each individual will become a normal part of preventative medicine in the future.

As more people have their genes mapped, researchers will develop treatments tailored to the individual patient by looking at his or her genes. This genetic testing would reveal which health problems you are likely to encounter. It would also show which drugs would work the best for you and would possibly allow the pharmacist to design a pill just for you – a pill that would prevent health problems, such as heart disease, diabetes or certain types of cancer, from beginning. After receiving your genetic roadmap, you might consult a doctor to discuss how your environment could

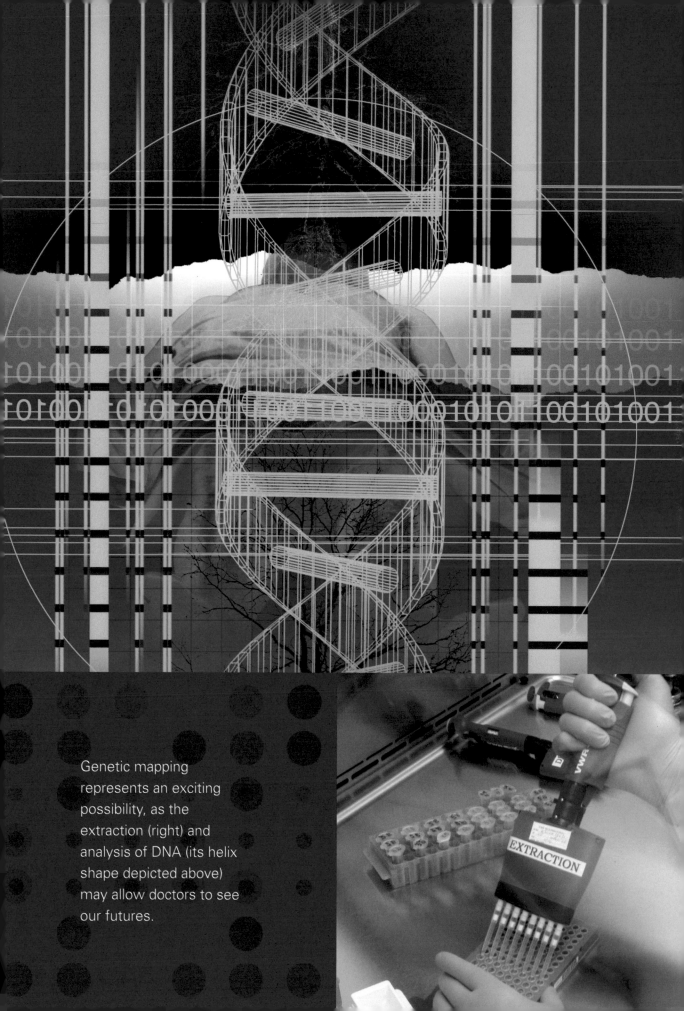

Genetic mapping represents an exciting possibility, as the extraction (right) and analysis of DNA (its helix shape depicted above) may allow doctors to see our futures.

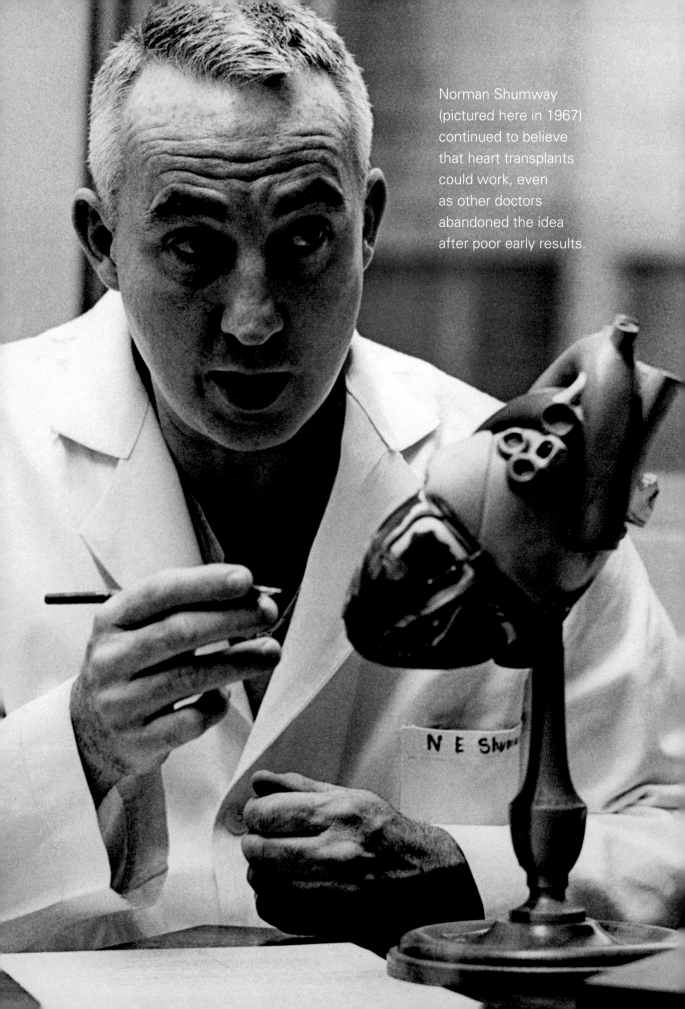

Norman Shumway (pictured here in 1967) continued to believe that heart transplants could work, even as other doctors abandoned the idea after poor early results.

THE TRANSPLANT AGE BEGINS

Norman Shumway and Richard Lower pioneered many of the techniques used in heart transplant surgery. The first human-to-human heart transplant was performed in 1967 by a South African surgeon called Christiaan Barnard, using Shumway and Lower's techniques. During the next few years, many surgeons performed heart transplants, but the procedures were usually unsuccessful, with patients dying from complications after only a few days or weeks. Shumway began using a new drug called cyclosporine, which helped prevent patients bodies from rejecting their new hearts. He also developed a procedure called a heart biopsy – removing a sample of tissue to check for disease – to treat a patient in the beginning stages of rejection before any complications could arise. Today, most heart donor recipients live at least five years with their new organs.

affect your genes, turning them on or off to cause diseases. Having this information could guide your lifestyle choices, such as the foods you eat or avoid. Or, for example, if your genes show that you are susceptible to developing skin cancer, you would know to take extra care in protecting your skin from the Sun's radiation.

Genetics could also play a role in future organ transplants. Scientists could take cells from newborn babies and store them for future use. If that child needed a new kidney or heart later in life, researchers could grow a new organ from the cells collected at birth. The patient's body would accept the organ because it came from the patient's own cells, avoiding the problem of rejection that many transplant patients experience today.

For people who had already developed clogged arteries or other forms of heart disease, it might be possible to grow new arteries and healthy heart muscle, eliminating the need for surgery. The doctor would inject drugs, either based on or made from stem cells, into the bloodstream. These drugs would travel to the heart and turn off the gene that prevents new cell growth. In heart attack patients, the cells would form new heart muscle to replace the cells that died from lack of oxygen. Within a few weeks, the patient's heart could be back to normal. In the same way, this type of drug could stimulate the growth of nerve cells to cure multiple sclerosis or cells in the retina to reverse macular degeneration.

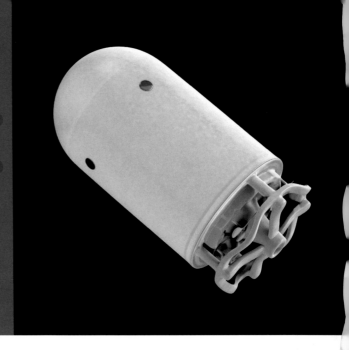

Cloning is a futuristic development that has already happened in the form of Dolly the sheep (pictured, opposite). Pill-sized medical nanobots (illustrated, right) may be coming.

In the future, patients who need surgery could undergo a procedure without any incisions being made on the outside of their bodies. First, the doctor would scan the patient's body to find the area in need of medical treatment. This scanning could be done with a small, handheld MRI (magnetic resonance imaging) device, about the size of a camera, instead of current MRI machines, which take up a small room. If the patient needed surgery, a robotic system called ARES (Assembling Reconfigurable Endoluminal Surgical system) might do the job from inside the patient's body. How would it get there? The patient would swallow up to 15 pill-sized pieces that would move through the body until they reached the surgery site and then assemble themselves into a working robot. Each piece would have a specific role to play in the procedure, such as communicating with a computer outside the body, taking diagnostic measurements, making incisions and taking samples to be examined after the operation. After an ARES operation, the patient would recover more quickly and with less pain than after traditional surgery because there would be fewer cuts to heal. The robot would either disintegrate in the body or follow the digestive system and leave the body naturally.

Even smaller robots and treatments will come from the field of nanotechnology. Nanotechnology involves structures that are so tiny they can interact with individual cells inside the body. A nanometre is one-billionth of a metre, a size so small it cannot be

THE CONTROVERSY OF CLONING

Cloning is a major source of controversy in medical research today. In the 1990s, researchers in Scotland cloned a sheep and created Dolly, a sheep that was identical to the original animal. The success of this experiment led to serious debates. Scientists believe that this technology may allow them to someday produce organs for transplant operations and healthy cells to replace the damaged ones in people with Alzheimer's or Parkinson's disease. But there are problems, too. Scientists have found that cloned animals, such as mice and cows, are prone to higher-than-normal rates of infection, disease and tumours. Some people also feel it is unethical for scientists to have such control over human life.

seen with any microscope yet developed. Equipped with cameras and sensors, tiny robots called nanobots will one day allow doctors to see how cells act inside the body and whether abnormal or diseased cells are present. Researchers predict many benefits of nanomedicine, and some even believe that medical pain and many common diseases, such as heart disease and infections, will no longer exist by the middle of the 21st century.

Today, when cancer patients undergo chemotherapy to kill their cancerous cells, the drugs kill some of their healthy cells, too. Nanotechnology could help deliver the necessary drugs without hurting healthy cells. To fight cancer, nanobots may one day search for cancerous cells. When they find one, they would analyse it and destroy it with a poison released to kill just that cell. If no cancer cells were detected, the nanobots would travel through the body as tiny guardians. People would no longer worry about their cancer returning, since, as soon as cancer cells began to form, the nanobots would detect and destroy them. Similarly, the nanobots might roam a patient's bloodstream, acting as an artificial immune system to identify infections and viruses. They would act more quickly than the body's white blood cells, and they could be programmed to fight new diseases. Nanobots could potentially also perform the most delicate operations, such as operating on a foetus, or unborn child, still in the womb.

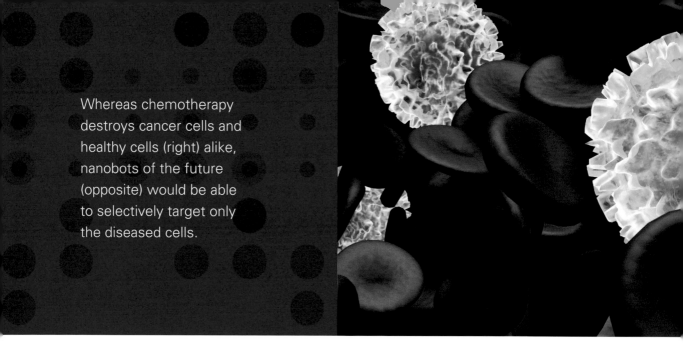

Whereas chemotherapy destroys cancer cells and healthy cells (right) alike, nanobots of the future (opposite) would be able to selectively target only the diseased cells.

Another use for nanomedicine may be in protecting our bodies against accident or injury. Having nanobots permanently placed in a person's skin could make the skin stronger, more resistant to damage and heal faster. Mixing nanomaterials with the body's cells could speed the regrowth of broken bones. Placed in a person's glands, nanobots might have the capability to jumpstart hormone production. Various hormone levels in our bodies decline as we age, and if nanobots could increase our hormone levels, they could reverse the effects of aging, and we might look and feel younger.

Nanotechnology is also helping bionics move forward. Some researchers predict that in as little as two decades, artificial limbs will be covered with artificial skin able to sense temperature and touch. Ultra-thin carbon nanotubes, only 1/10,000th as thick as a human hair, would cover the skin in the same way that human hair grows from skin, and function to conduct heat and electricity to a person's nerves. This technology might also help replace damaged skin in burn victims.

SCIENCE FICTION TO MEDICAL FACT

Avoiding a disease by undergoing gene repair, or having tiny machines swim through our bodies in search of cancerous cells sound like the plot of a science-fiction film. However, scientists believe that with years of research and steady advancements in technology, they can overcome potential problems or fears about these new types of treatment, making them standard practice in the medical community.

Many genetic diseases are caused by problems in more than one gene. Sometimes, environmental factors can trigger the genes to cause diseases. To better understand how this happens, researchers in several countries, including Sweden and the United Kingdom, have recruited thousands of volunteers for their biobanks. In the United Kingdom, 500,000 people have agreed to donate their DNA and have their medical records tracked for the rest of their lives. The principal investigator for the project, Rory Collins, Professor of Medicine and Epidemiology at Oxford University, said that to find out how genes work together and work with the environment, "... you need to do studies that are very, very big. It's only just now that the technology allows those experiments to be done."

Armed with enough blood samples to fill two oil tankers and the promise of being able to track changes as volunteers return for future check-ups, researchers hope to unlock the secrets behind widespread medical problems such as arthritis, heart disease and diabetes. They hope the results will reveal trends in how a person's environment – which includes what people eat, where they work, the

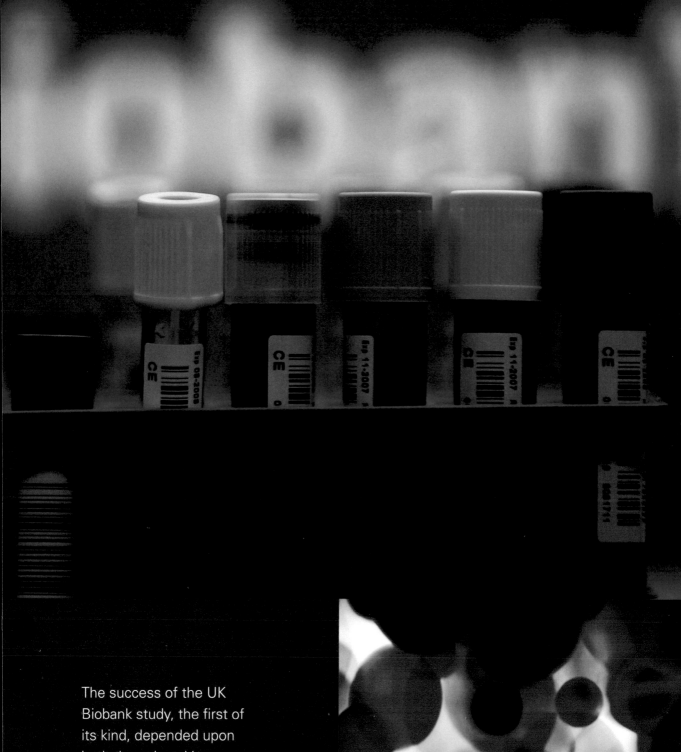

The success of the UK
Biobank study, the first of
its kind, depended upon
both the painstaking
work of researchers and
the truthfulness of the
answers provided by
donors.

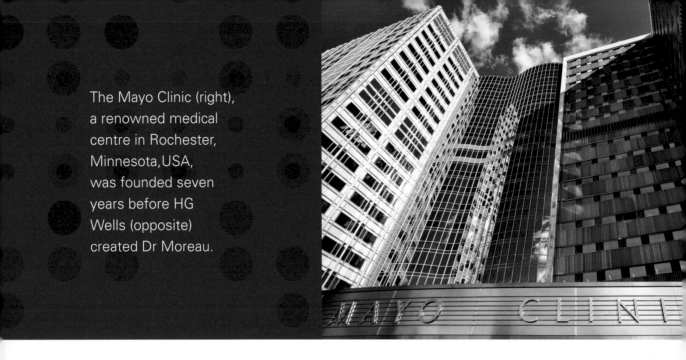

The Mayo Clinic (right), a renowned medical centre in Rochester, Minnesota,USA, was founded seven years before HG Wells (opposite) created Dr Moreau.

pollution or chemicals to which they are exposed, and other factors – may have an impact on the development of diseases. In the United States, the Mayo Clinic began collecting blood and tissue samples in 2009 as part of a three-year project to enroll 20,000 of its patients into the project.

The problem with collecting enormous quantities of data is that the human brain, and even today's fastest computers, cannot sort and fully analyse all of it. Machines that sequence the human genome produce billions of bits of data. Before gene mapping can become a common practice in healthcare, it will need to be quick and easy to do, and the results must have clear meaning for doctors and patients. In the future, researchers hope that computer programs will be able to glean all the information from a genome and neatly summarise it. Much progress has already been made since the first genome was sequenced. Researchers spent 13 years creating that map. With new companies competing to perfect gene mapping, and with improvements in computer capabilities, genome sequencing will take less and less time.

To make nanomachines a reality, scientists will need to work out how to take the obvious but challenging first step – building them. Today, researchers are attempting to develop the various parts of nanodevices. Across the world, people working in the field of nanomedicine are studying how cells and molecules operate to understand how nanodevices will interact with them. Nanobots will

WELLS FORESHADOWS GENETIC EXPERIMENTS

In 1896, English science-fiction author HG Wells wrote The Island of Dr Moreau.
In the novel, the mysterious Dr Moreau lives on a secluded island, where he performs vivisections, or operations on live animals, to create half-human, half-animal creatures. Although such studies have never been legitimately done in real life, scientists have used animals in medical research and testing for many years. Tropical fish have been genetically altered to glow in the dark. Cattle, sheep, goats and pigs have been used in cloning experiments. Researchers have investigated ways to change the genes of these animals so that they will produce human proteins that might one day be used to cure people.

PASTEUR'S GERM-KILLING PROCESS

During the 19th century, while scientists were beginning to believe that germs caused disease, a French chemist and microbiologist named Louis Pasteur was devising a way to kill germs. He believed that if doctors boiled their medical instruments and steamed the bandages, the heat would destroy the germs on the objects and reduce infections among patients. He applied his ideas to perishable foods and also discovered that sealing containers shut bacteria out. His process of heating (mostly liquid) foods to kill bacteria became known as pasteurisation, and it is still used to extend the shelf life of milk, orange juice and other foods.

need much smaller and faster computers than are currently available. Instead of building computers out of silicon chips as they do now, researchers might use nanochips, built atom by atom. It is a daunting process, but each year brings new advances. Just a few decades ago, a single computer filled an entire room; today, such a machine would be dwarfed in power by a computer smaller than a notebook. It is therefore possible to imagine that nanocomputers will become a reality in the not-so-distant future.

Because nanobots will be incredibly small, it could take millions of them to perform the tasks for which they are designed. Rather than building each one, scientists might design nanobots so that they can replicate themselves. How big should they be and how fast should they move? Nanobots will need a source of energy to perform their jobs and researchers have yet to work out how to power such microscopic machines.

Despite the potential advantages of nanomedicine and other medical advances, patients might not embrace these new kinds of treatment. Scientists will need to consider and overcome the dangers and ethical dilemmas posed by these areas of research. For example, if nanobots are designed to multiply inside the body, what if they don't stop? What happens if they stop working? Also, some people might worry that this technology could be used to cause damage and might be put to sinister use. Could nanobots be designed to dismantle blood cells, bones or organs, one molecule at a time – essentially becoming terrifying weapons?

Like nanomedicine, genetic manipulation is a controversial area of research marked by many questions. Many researchers and corporations today are attempting to improve plants, animals and food with genetic engineering. They have made certain crops resistant to disease, and they have modified the genes of some

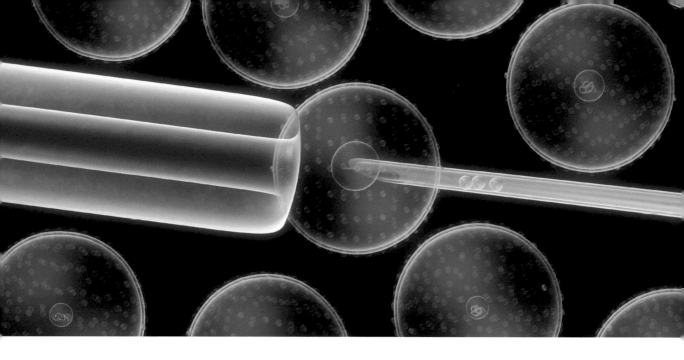

cows so that the animals produce more milk, or milk with different
nutrients in it. But experiments in gene research can also lead
to mistakes, including potentially fatal ones. In 2001, a group of
scientists created a genetically modified virus to prevent mice from
having babies. Instead, the virus killed the mice. Some scientists
might intentionally create genetically modified viruses specifically
designed to harm people. If countries develop such bio-weapons,
warfare will become even more dangerous.

Some experts are against modifying human genes and using stem
cells for ethical reasons. Once scientists are able to 'fix' genes to help
people avoid getting ill, they will probably be able to identify specific
genes that parents want for their babies. Of course, no one wants their
children to develop diseases, but how much control is too much? Should
parents be able to create 'designer babies', choosing their child's genes
to maximise their appearance, intelligence or athletic ability? In the USA
in 2013 the first baby was born that had been genetically screened to
see whether it had any faulty chromosomes, before the mother was
implanted with the embryo during IVF treatment. Also, when a patient
has his or her genome mapped in the future, it will probably reveal the
natural causes that may lead to the person's death. Employers who have
access to such information about potential employees might not hire
certain people. Insurance companies might refuse to offer coverage to
people depending on their predicted cause of death. Countries will need
to establish regulations for dealing with these complicated issues.

CUSTOM-MADE BABIES DELIVERED

Doc's design-a-kid offer creates a flap

A FERTILITY CLINIC'S promise to deliver the ultimate in designer babies — letting parents choose eye, hair and even skin color — is sparking a worldwide uproar.

BY GINA SALAMONE
DAILY NEWS STAFF WRITER

Dr. Jeff Steinberg has already let thousands decide their kids' gender. Now he says that within the next six months, the Manhattan and L.A. offices of his Fertility Institutes will let would-be moms and dads pick whether junior has blue or brown eyes or black or blond hair.

"In the process of doing gender selection . . . we've also uncovered the technology [to] characterize things like eye and hair color," said Steinberg, 54.

The idea of a Build-A-Bear style baby was slammed yesterday by bioethicists and right-to-life groups — and Pope Benedict has warned against it for years.

The Pope railed against the "obsessive search for the perfect child" just two weekends ago. "A new mentality is creeping in that tends to justify a different consideration of life and personal dignity," he said.

Steinberg countered that reproductive technologies aren't about to go away.

"Genetic health is the wave of the future," he said. "It's already happening and it's not going to go away. It's going to expand. So if they've got major problems with it, they need to sit down and really examine their own consciences because there's nothing that's going to stop it."

Custom-made kids will be achieved through preimplantation genetic diagnosis, or PGD, the procedure used to weed out problem embryos and to allow parents to choose a gender.

In letting parents decide what traits their kids have, doctors will examine the genetic makeup of embryos created in the lab and implant the ones that have the best chance of giving mom and dad what they want.

Some doctors question Steinberg's ability to give parents their pick of traits.

"He's the only one offering this because you can't yet do it," said Sean Tipton of the American Society for Reproductive Technology. "Nobody can do this right now."

Dr. William Kearns, head of the Shady Grove Center for Preimplantation Genetics in Rockville, Md., disagrees. His research has identified genes relating to northern European skin, hair and eye pigmentation, but he won't use it to let parents design their kids.

Steinberg, one of the doctors who helped produce the first test-tube baby, admits the technology isn't 100% — and says for now the best results are with couples of Scandinavian heritage.

"Say you mean seven embryos, and one of them has got the highest chance of green eyes, and that chance is 80%. It's not perfect science because eye and hair color are not perfect genetics," said Steinberg, who opened an office on E. 40th St. two months ago.

There are no laws in New York that address how PGD testing can be used. Opponents say there should be.

Lori Kehoe, executive director of the New York State Right to Life Committee, is upset that the embryos deemed undesirable will be destroyed.

She said it is "sickening to flush a member of the human family down the drain" because they are not considered perfect.

Prof. Alexander Capron, bioethicist and professor of law and medicine at the University of Southern California, called Steinberg's practice problematic. "The notion of unconditional love and support — which is assumed to be what parents owe their children — is totally undermined here," he said.

"You're saying I want to order up just what I want and that's what I'll love."

One New York doctor even likened it to the pursuit of a master race.

"We're crossing the line into eugenics, the theory of trying to give people enhanced characteristics — genetic engineering to make sort of the superman or superwoman," said Dr. Daniel Sulmasy, director of ethics at New York Medical College and St. Vincent's Hospital.

With Nancy Dillon in Los Angeles and Nicole Lyn Pesce in New York
gsalamone@nydailynews.com

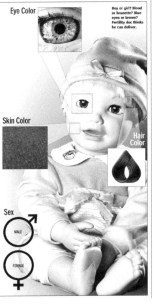

Eye Color

Skin Color

Hair Color

Sex

MALE

FEMALE

Boy or girl? Blond or brunette? Blue eyes or brown? Fertility doc thinks he can deliver.

Jeff Steinberg

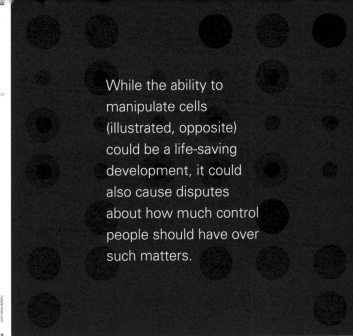

While the ability to manipulate cells (illustrated, opposite) could be a life-saving development, it could also cause disputes about how much control people should have over such matters.

Regardless of whether researchers use adult or embryonic stem cells, they will need to do further studies before this treatment can be considered a safe option. Studies of stem cells injected into mice and other test animals have shown that the stem cells that do not migrate to the desired location in the body can build up in other areas and form cancerous tumours. Researchers will also need to find better ways of preventing the body from attacking unrecognised cells and tissues taken from other people.

Before doctors can treat people with new drugs or medical devices, the treatments must be proved safe and effective. In the UK, the Medicines and Healthcare Products Regulatory Agency regulates new medicines and medical devices and approves the ones that meet specific standards. New treatments must go through many rounds of testing, which could take months or years to complete. Still, with research already underway in many areas, medicine could be very different in 20 years time from what it is today. Doctors will need to be prepared to use the latest advances in medicine, which means that medical schools may need to alter their teaching methods.

Medicine has advanced rapidly in the past 500 years. Today, in the early part of the 21st century, scientists are looking at this area with a new purpose. No longer content just to understand and treat diseases, many now aspire to be able to prevent disease with genetic mapping and nanorobotics. Although challenges remain, the world of medicine will undoubtedly change, perhaps sooner than we think.

GLOSSARY

anaesthetic a drug that makes a patient lose sensation or consciousness before an operation begins

archaeologists people who study material remains such as artefacts, buildings and bones to learn about past human life

bacteria microscopic living things, some of which casue diseases

biobanks collections of stored biological materials, such as human tissue or blood samples, and clinical information about the donors of the materials

chemotherapy the treatment of a disease (usually cancer) using chemicals or drugs that selectively destroy diseased cells or whatever is causing the disease

cloning the process of creating one or more genetic duplicates of a single organism by artificial or controlled means

degenerative describing a condition that causes the body or part of the body to become weaker or less able to function as time passes

developed countries the wealthiest countries of the world, which are generally characterised by good healthcare, nutrition, education and industry

disintegrate to break into many small parts or pieces

electrodes conductors through which an electric current enters or leaves a substance; they can be used to detect electrical activity, such as brain waves, in the body

epidemic an occurrence in which a disease spreads very quickly and affects a large number of people

epidemiology the study of patterns of health and illness and how they spread though and affect a population

genes hereditary units that determine the particular characteristics of an organism

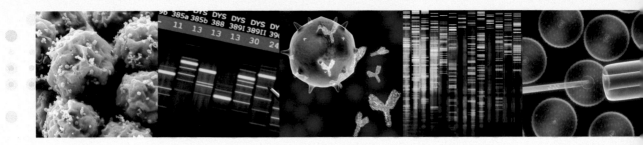

glands organs in the body that draw certain substances from blood and alter them into new substances that help the body function

hereditary describing traits that are passed from parents to children before birth

hormone a natural substance that is produced in the body and that influences the way the body grows or develops

immune system the collection of biological structures (such as white blood cells) and processes that a body uses to fight disease

incision a cut made into a body during surgery

laxatives food or drugs that stimulate bowel movements

macular degeneration a gradual loss of the central part of a person's field of vision, usually affecting both eyes and occurring especially in the elderly

parasitic describing an organism that grows and feeds on or in a different organism while contributing nothing to its host

prosthesis an artificial device that replaces or assists a missing or impaired part of the body

proteins substances responsible for the growth and repair of tissues in human and animal bodies

replicate to duplicate, or produce an identical or near-identical copy

stroke a serious medical condition caused by the sudden stoppage of blood flow to the brain; it can result in long-term brain damage or physical problems

vaccination the administration of a specially prepared dose of tiny organisms such as viruses as a means of making the body increase its ability to fight a particular disease

virus contagious or poisionous matter that can cause infctions and diseases

FURTHER READING

Cloning and Genetic Engineering (Both Sides of the Story) by Nicola
 Barber (Franklin Watts, 2013)
Future Science Now (What's Next for Medicine?) by Tom Jackson
 (Wayland, 2013)
Human Body (Super Science) by Rob Coulson (Franklin Watts, 2013)
Robots in Medicine and Science (Robot World) by Steve Parker
 (Franklin Watts, 2011)
The Usborne Introduction to Genes & DNA by Anna Claybourne,
 (Usborne Publishing, 2006)

WEBSITES

HowStuffWorks: How Designer Children Work
*http://science.howstuffworks.com/environmental/life/genetic/
designer-children.htm*
This site provides a detailed but accessible explanation of the human
genome and discusses how genetic mapping may make it possible
for parents to 'design' children.

UK Biobank
http://www.ukbiobank.ac.uk/
Learn more about the UK Biobank study at this site. Among other
topics, it explains how a giant freezer facility was built to store the
study's ten million blood samples.

INDEX

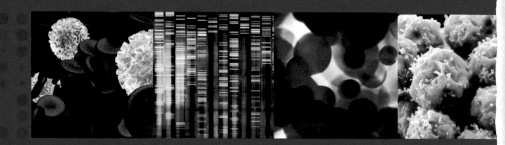

First published in the UK in 2013 by

Franklin Watts
338 Euston Road
London NW1 3BH

First published by Creative Education
P.O. Box 227, Mankato, Minnesota 56002
Creative Education is an imprint of The Creative Company
www.thecreativecompany.us
Copyright © 2013 Creative Education
ISBN: 978 1 4451 2377 6
Dewey number: 610.2'8

A CIP catalogue record for this book is available from the British Library.

Printed in China

Franklin Watts is a division of Hachette Children's Books,
 an Hachette Uk Company
www.hachette.co.uk

Design and production by The Design Lab
Art direction by Rita Marshall

Photographs by Alamy (AF Archive, Everett Collection Inc., INTERFOTO, Mic Smith
Photography LCC, Jeremy Sutton-Hibbert), Bigstock (biopic, danilo2, Eraxion, Flogel,
kentoh, krishnacreations), Corbis (Bettmann/Corbis, Steve Gschmeissner/Science
Photo Library, Hulton-Deutsch Collection/Corbis, Jason Reed/Reuters), Dreamstime
(Alexstar, Billyfoto, Cornelius20, Diego Vito Cervo, Vasily Kaleda, Stanislav Perov,
Pictureguy66, Pseudolongino, Nurbek Sagynbaev, Skyhawk911, Serghei Starus, Tallik,
Xalanx), Getty Images (Christopher Furlong, Sean Gallup, NY Daily News Archive,
Popperfoto), iStockphoto (dra_schwartz, Gunnar Assmy, Pgiam)

Cover: A digital illustration of the influenza virus
Page 1: A hospital patient being X-rayed in 1933
Page 2: A digital illustration of DNA data